Grade 1

Science Resources

Developed at
The Lawrence Hall of Science,
University of California, Berkeley
Published and distributed by
Delta Education,
a member of the School Specialty Family

1361721
978-1-60902-491-8
Printing 1 — 5/2013
Courier, Kendallville, IN

Physical Science
Solids and Liquids

Table of Contents

Earth Science

Rocks, Soil, and Air

Life Science

Plants and Animals

References

Physical Science
Solids and Liquids

Table of Contents

Everything Matters

The world is made up of many things. Trees, bubbles, slides, and drinking fountains are just some of them. These things may all seem very different. But in one way, they are all the same. They are all **matter**. Matter is anything that takes up space.

Matter can be divided into three groups called
states. They are **solid**, **liquid**, and **gas**.

A slide is a solid.

Water is a liquid.

Bubbles are filled with **air**. Air is a gas. How did the gas get into the bubbles?

Gases are hard to see and feel. You can't hold gas in your hand or see it in a bucket. How can you see gas?

Air is gas, and air is all around. You can see air make a windmill spin. Which windmills show air at work?

A helium balloon is fun. Helium is a kind of gas.
It is lighter than air. What happens when you let
go of a helium balloon? It floats away.

We use solids and liquids all the time.
Every solid and liquid is different. So
they are useful in different ways.

Cement bricks are strong and hard.
They are just right for building walls.

Wool is soft and flexible. It is good
for hats and scarves.

Water can spray and splash. It makes
a hot summer day lots of fun!

Look around you for solids and liquids.
How will you use them today?

Solid Objects and Materials

Chairs are solid **objects**.
Blocks are solid objects.
So are chopsticks.

Chairs, blocks, and chopsticks are all different.
We sit on chairs. We build with blocks. We eat
with chopsticks.

Chairs, blocks, and chopsticks are all the same,
too. They are all made of the same **material**.
They are all made of wood.

Wood has good **properties** for making chairs.
Wood is strong and rigid.

But wood is not a good material for making socks.
What material has good properties for socks?

Fabric is a good material for socks. Fabric is soft
and flexible. Fabric is a good material for shirts
and blankets, too.

Kick balls are solid objects. Rubber is a good material for kick balls. Rubber stretches, and it is strong.

Rubber is a good material for making tires and balloons, too.

Shoes are solid objects. This shoe is made of three different materials. Can you see all three materials?

Some shoes are made of fabric, rubber, and metal. Some shoes are made of the material leather. Leather is strong and flexible.

Jars are solid objects. This jar is made of two materials. Can you see the two materials?

The jar is made of the material plastic. Plastic is strong and light. The label is made of the material paper. Paper is light and flexible.

Windows are solid objects. Windows are made of the material glass. Glass is strong and transparent.

What other objects are made of glass?

Cars are solid objects. Cars are made of
many materials. How many different
materials can you see?

Review Questions

1. What material would be good for making an umbrella? Tell about the material's properties.

2. How many materials are used to make a pencil? Tell about the properties of each material.

3. Name two properties you can use to sort objects.

4. How are materials different from objects?

Towers

A **tower** is a tall structure. This is an airport control tower. It is rigid and has a wide base. The base helps the tower stand by itself.

You can see the whole airport from the top of the tower!

This is a bridge tower. It is rigid and has
a wide base.

It is tall to hold a road over the water below.
Bridge towers help people cross rivers and bays.

This is a communication tower. It is rigid, but it does not have a wide base.

It can stand by itself. A strong, steel frame keeps the tower from falling over.

This structure is called the Space Needle. It is tall and rigid. It has a wide base. Do you think it is a tower?

Liquids

They can splash. They can squirt. They can bubble and fizz. They come in many colors. What are they? Liquids!

Liquids can spill. Liquids can flow. That's why liquids have to be kept in containers. Glasses, bottles, and tank trucks are containers.

Do you know what the largest liquid
container in the world is? It's the ocean!

Liquids flow. That's why they can change shape.
These four glasses are the same size and shape.
Each glass has the same amount of liquid.

These containers are different sizes and shapes.
Let's pour liquid from three of the glasses into
the containers.

The water looks different! It is a different shape.
The same amount of water can be tall and thin.
It can be short and wide.

Liquids change shape in each kind of container.

Liquids always move to the bottom of a container.
The liquid is in the bottom of this bottle.

Look at the pictures of the bottle turning over.
Compare pictures 1 and 3. Did the liquid move?
Or did the bottle move? What is different about
the liquid in all the pictures?

What is the same about the liquid in all the pictures? Look at the line near the surface of the liquid. It doesn't matter how you turn the bottle. The surface is always flat and level.

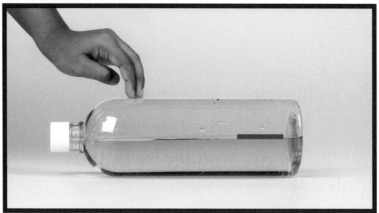

Pouring

Rocks are solid objects. This mountain is a giant rock. Boulders are big rocks. River rocks and gravel are smaller rocks that you can pick up.

A piece of sand is a tiny rock. We call pieces of sand **particles**. You can put millions of sand particles in a bucket.

Sand can pour out of a bucket. Is sand a liquid or a solid?

The **surface** of a liquid is always flat
and level. Is the surface of sand flat?
Is the surface of sand level?

Heavy, solid objects **sink** in liquids. Do heavy objects sink in sand?

What happens when you pour sand and water on a hard surface? The sand makes a pile. But the water flows and spreads out.

Review Questions

Here are some materials that pour.

1. Are they solids or liquids?

2. What properties help you decide?

Comparing Solids and Liquids

What is the difference between solids and liquids? They have different properties. Properties describe how something looks or feels.

Shape and size are two properties of solid objects. The shape and size don't change unless you do something to the objects. Solids can be rigid, like a bat. When something is rigid, you can't bend it.

Solids can be flexible, like a sweater.
When something is flexible, you can
bend and stretch it.

Some solids can be broken into pieces. Each piece has a different shape and takes up less space.

What happens when you put the pieces back together? The solid has the same shape as before. It takes up the same space, too.

Solid objects can be very small, like sand. You
can pour sand out of a bucket. But every grain
of sand is a solid.

Liquids have properties, too. A liquid can be poured. It doesn't have its own shape. It takes the shape of the container that holds it.

A liquid has a different shape in each different container.

Liquids can be **foamy, bubbly,** or **transparent.**
They can be **translucent** or **viscous**.

viscous

translucent

foamy

bubbly and transparent

Solids and liquids are all around you. Can you find the solids in each picture? Can you find the liquids?

Review Questions

1. What are properties?

2. Tell about the properties of solids.

3. Tell about the properties of liquids.

4. What properties can you use to sort solids and liquids?

Mix It Up!

When you put together two or more things,
you get a **mixture**.

Can you see what things make up this mixture?

What happens when you mix two liquids?

It depends. Sometimes the liquids mix together to make one new liquid.

Sometimes they don't mix. The two liquids form layers.

What happens when you mix a solid with
a liquid?

It depends. Solids like marbles just get wet.
A solid like a cookie falls apart. It breaks
into smaller pieces.

A solid like salt disappears in a liquid.
It **dissolves**. The salt breaks apart into
tiny pieces. The pieces are so small you
can't see them.

How can you find out if the salt is there? If you wait long enough, the liquid will **evaporate**. The water will go into the air. The salt is left behind in the form of **crystals**.

Solids and liquids are everywhere. We use them every day. How are solids being used here?

How are liquids being used here?

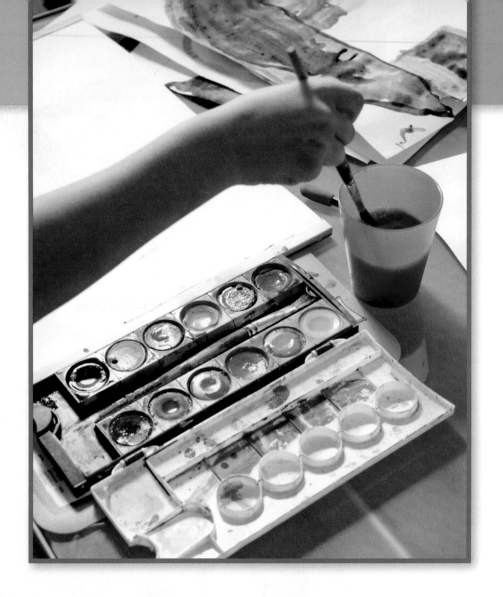

Review Questions

1. Tell about a mixture of solids.

2. Tell about a mixture of liquids.

3. Tell about a mixture of solids and liquids.

4. Tell what changes happen to salt and water when you mix them.

Heating and Cooling

Have you ever had a glass of lemonade on a hot summer day? After you drink the lemonade, ice is left in the glass. What do you **predict** happens next? After a while, the ice turns to water. The ice **melts**.

When a solid melts, it changes from a
solid to a liquid.

Other solids can melt, too. Butter is a
solid. But if you **heat** the butter, it melts.
Solids melt when they get hot.

Liquids can change to solids, too. Do you know how?

Think about making ice cubes. You pour water in a tray. Then, you put it in a cold place. When the water gets very cold, you have solid ice cubes! When a liquid **cools** or **freezes**, it changes to a solid.

Can you think of other liquids that turn to solid?

Liquid chocolate turns to solid as it cools. Liquid chocolate can be poured into molds. When the chocolate cools, it is solid. That's how candy is made into different shapes!

This candle is melting and freezing at the same time. The wax near the flame gets hot. It melts and turns to liquid. The liquid wax flows down the side of the candle. When the liquid wax is away from the heat, it cools and freezes.

Review Questions

1. Tell about how solids change into liquids.

2. Tell about how liquids change into solids.

3. Look at the ice in the picture above. What do you predict will happen to the ice on a sunny day? Why do you think so?

4. What do you predict will happen to water outside on a cold winter day? Why do you think so?

Magnets and Force

Look at the **magnets** on the pencil. What do you see? What do you think is happening?

Magnetism is a force. The magnetic force can push and pull other magnets. One magnet can make another magnet move. The magnets don't even have to touch!

Magnets also pull on metals like iron and steel. Here's a way to use a magnet to move something without touching it. Hang a paper clip from a string. Use a magnet to lift the paper clip. How high can you lift the paper clip without touching it?

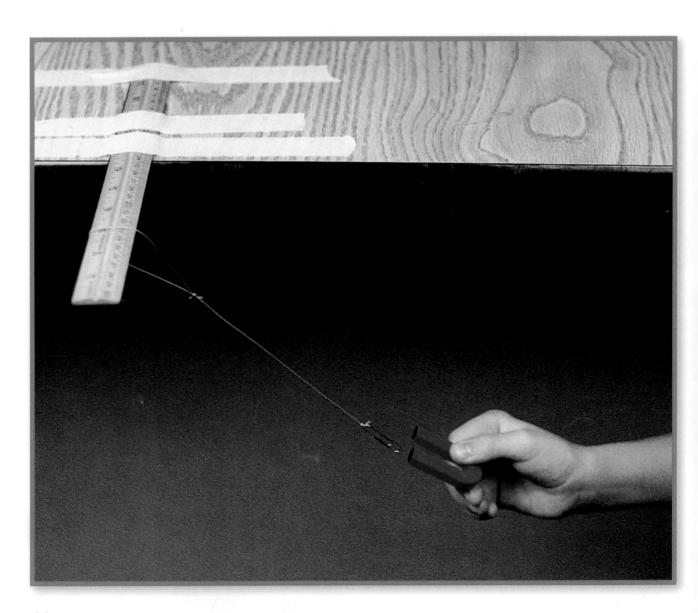

Here is a toy that uses magnets. The toy has
magnets on each end of the train cars. Magnetic
fields keep the trains together as you move them.
When you pull on the train engine, the magnet
pulls on the train car behind it.

Review Questions

1. Think about a paper clip on top of a table. Tell about three ways to move the paper clip.

2. What is a way to move the paper clip without touching it?

3. What do you predict will happen if you move a magnet near a steel nail?

4. Is magnetism a force? Why or why not?

The Way Things Move

Things can move by rolling. When something **rolls**, it goes around and around. But instead of staying in one spot, it moves from one place to another.

Things that have round surfaces roll easily. Marbles roll, and so do cans.

Some things **spin**. When something spins, it turns on its **axis**. Look at the wheels on this page. Are the wheels spinning or rolling?

Some things don't roll in a straight line. Things that are shaped like a paper cup don't roll straight.

Some things don't roll at all. Things that are flat won't roll.

Which of these things will roll down the ramp?

Gravity helps things roll downhill. It's
fun to see how fast something will go.

Which ramp would you use? Why?

Ready, set, go!

Things move in different ways. Some things spin. They go around and around. Some things roll. They go around and ahead.

Things can move closer to us. Things can move farther away.

Some things bounce. They go up
and down.

Some things rock or sway. They go back and forth.

Some things move fast, and some move slow.

Look at these pictures.
How do these objects move?

Fast, slow, up, down, spinning, rolling, sliding . . .
Almost everything moves!

What ways can you move?

Review Questions

1. Name four things that roll.

2. What are the different ways objects can move?

3. A friend kicks a ball. Tell what happens. Where does the ball go? How does it move?

4. What is the difference between rolling and spinning?

Earth Science
Rocks, Soil, and Air

Table of Contents

Exploring Rocks

Think about a **rock**. A rock has many **properties**. What does the rock look like?

Rocks can be small or large. They can be heavy or light. They can be smooth or rough. They can be round or flat, shiny or dull. Rocks can be different in many ways.

Some rocks are too big to hold in your hand. A rock can be as big as a mountain!

Other rocks are so small that you can hold thousands in your hand. Look at the picture of a **sand** dune. Can you see the tiny rocks blowing in the wind?

Rocks of all sizes can be found in rivers.
Over time, rocks in a river become smooth.
Rocks become smooth from rubbing against
one another.

Rocks of all sizes can be found in a desert, too.
How big is the rock you're thinking of?

Rocks can be many different colors. They can be black, brown, red, or white. They might even be pink or green. Some rocks have speckles or stripes, too.

Rocks can be many different sizes. They can have different **textures**. They can be many colors and shapes. They can even have patterns.

What does the rock you're thinking about look like?

Review Questions

1. The author said to think about a rock.
Describe the rock you were thinking about.

2. What are some properties of rocks?

Colorful Rocks

What are these colorful objects?

They are **minerals**. There are many different kinds of minerals. Minerals come in lots of different colors.

Rocks are made out of minerals. That's why
rocks can be so many different colors.

This rock is made of different minerals. Can you see them?

Look for the black mineral. Look for the pink mineral. Look for the gray mineral. These are the minerals in this rock. This rock is called pink **granite**.

The Story of Sand

Have you ever looked at one grain of sand
and thought, "I wonder how it got so small?"

A grain of sand wasn't always so small! It might have once been part of a **boulder**. The boulder could have broken off a mountain. The boulder could have tumbled down the mountain.

Maybe the boulder rolled into a river. Water in a river can move rocks. The rocks bump together in the water. The boulder might have broken into **cobbles** and **pebbles**. Cobbles are bigger than pebbles.

Maybe the river carried the pebbles to the ocean. Ocean waves crash over pebbles. The pebbles might have broken into **gravel**. Pebbles are bigger than gravel.

Wind and water move and rub rocks together.
Over time, rocks break apart. They can get
smaller and smaller. They can break into very
tiny rocks. This is called **weathering**. These
tiny rocks are grains of sand.

Compare the sand from different places.

Corpus Christi, Texas

Dawson City, Texas

Green Sands Bay, Hawaii

Plum Island, Massachusetts

**Cape Hatteras National
Seashore, North Carolina**

Dix Beach, North Carolina

100

Next time you build a sand castle,
think about the story of sand!

Review Questions

1. Put these rocks in order by size, from the largest to the smallest.

> sand
>
> boulder
>
> gravel
>
> cobble
>
> pebble

2. Tell the story of sand.

Rocks Move

Water and wind move rocks of all sizes.

Look at the picture. Can you tell what moved the rocks?

Mudflat

Sandy beach

Can you tell what moved these rocks?

Washout

Making Things with Rocks and Water

People use rocks and water to make useful
things. A quarry is a place where people
dig rocks out of the ground.

Big pieces of rock are used to make big things.
Statues and churches are often made from rock.
People make things out of rock because it lasts
a long time.

Pebbles and gravel are part of the mixture called **asphalt**. Asphalt is used to pave streets and playgrounds.

Gravel and sand are used to make sidewalks. The gravel and sand are mixed together with **cement** and water. Cement is like glue. It holds the mixture together. When the mixture gets hard, it makes **concrete**.

Even the tiniest rocks are useful. **Clay** is made up of rocks that are tinier than sand! They are so small that you can't see only one rock with your eyes. People mold wet clay into many shapes.

Clay is used to make bricks. Bricks are used to
make walls and buildings. Bricks are used to
make walking paths, too.

The bricks are held together with concrete **mortar**. Look at the mortar between the bricks. It is made of cement and sand.

Some bricks are made of concrete. They are called cinder blocks. How are cinder blocks and bricks the same? How are they different?

Whatever their size, rocks are important. People make useful and beautiful things from rocks.

Review Questions

1. What was made of rock in the reading?

2. What do rocks and water help people do?

3. Think about the things in your home and school.
What things were made using rocks or water?
What evidence can you find?

What Are Natural Resources?

Rocks, soil, and water are **natural resources**. They are useful earth materials. Rock walls can be formed by nature. Rock walls can be made by people, too.

Look at the rock walls. Which ones are natural? Which ones are made by people?

Stepping stones and walking paths can be natural. Stepping stones and walking paths can be made by people, too.

Look at the walking paths. Which ones are natural? Which ones are made by people?

Rock gardens can be natural. Rock gardens can be made by people, too.

Look at the rock gardens. Which ones are natural? Which ones are made by people?

119

What Is in Soil?

Rocks are all around you. The **soil** under your feet has rocks in it. The rocks are different sizes. Some of the tiny rocks and minerals in soil are called **silt**. Silt is smaller than sand, but bigger than clay. Sand, clay, gravel, and pebbles can be in soil, too.

When plants and animals die, they become part of the soil. Plants and animals **decay** into tiny pieces called **humus**. Humus provides **nutrients** for plants. It also helps the soil **retain** water.

What is this animal that lives in soil? A worm!
Worms are good for soil. They burrow through
the soil. They break it apart and enrich the
humus. Worms help plants grow by mixing
and turning the soil.

Not all soil is alike. Some soil has more humus. Some has more clay or sand. Some has more pebbles and gravel. What differences do you see in these soils?

The properties of soil depend on what makes up
the soil. We can describe soil by its properties of
color, texture, and particle size. Soil with lots of
humus looks black. Some soil looks tan.

Sandy soil feels gritty. Silty soil feels smooth.
Sandy soil has larger particles than silty soil.
Silty soil has larger particles than clay soil.

Soil and water help us make useful things, too. People use soil and water to grow plants. Some plants are used for food. Some plants are used for clothing or medicine. Trees are plants we use for wood and paper.

Review Questions

1. How do these soils compare with the soils you have observed?

2. What are three properties of soil?

3. What do soil and water help people do?

4. What things are made using soil and water? What evidence can you find?

Testing Soil

Do plants grow better in soil or sand? Here's what you can do to find out.

1. Get four cups that are all the same size.

2. Fill two cups with potting soil that has lots of humus. Fill the other two cups with sand.

3. Plant three sunflower seeds in each cup.

4. Put the same amount of water in each cup.

5. Keep the cups in a sunny window, and record what happens.

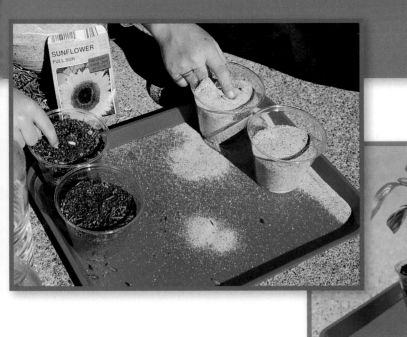

Review Questions

1. Is this a good way to test whether plants grow better in soil or sand?

2. Two students planted seeds in soil and sand. Look at the plants above. Which seeds grew better? Why do you think that happened?

3. Do the test yourself. Record and organize your data. Use pictures, numbers, and words. Tell about your observations. What did you find out?

Where Is Water Found?

Water is found everywhere on
Earth. Water is part of every living
thing. Every plant and animal is
made of water. Even you are
made mostly of water!

Fresh water is found in streams
and rivers. Streams can be small
like a creek. Rivers are larger
streams of water.

Streams and rivers bring water
into and out of ponds and lakes.

Fresh water is found in ponds and lakes, too.
Ponds are small bodies of water. Lakes are larger
and deeper bodies of water.

The water moves slowly in ponds and lakes. Sand
and silt settle to the bottom of ponds and lakes.

Fresh water is our most important natural resource. Plants and animals need water to live and grow. People use water to drink, cook, and wash. People use water to grow food and to power factories, too.

Most of the water on Earth is **salt water**.
Salt water is found in seas and the ocean.
The ocean is the largest body of salt water.
Seas are smaller than the ocean.

Salt water is found in salt **marshes**. They are
muddy places next to seas. Salt marshes have
lots of grasses and small plants. Salt marshes
have slow-moving water.

Salt water is found in mangrove **forests**.
They are like salt marshes, but they have
trees and bushes. The roots of mangrove
trees help protect the shore.

Salt water is found in coral reefs. Coral reefs grow in warm, shallow seas. Coral reefs are made from corals. Corals are the hard parts of sea animals.

Salt water is found on sandy beaches and rocky shores, too. You can see the ocean water move back and forth in waves on beaches and shores.

Where is fresh water found in your community?
Where is salt water found in your community?

Review Questions

1. Where is fresh water found?
Name and describe the places.

2. How do we use fresh water?

3. Where is salt water found?
Name and describe the places.

States of Water

Liquid water is one state of water. We can pour it into a glass to drink. We spray it from a hose to water plants. Liquid water can drip from a fountain.

We see liquid water as dewdrops in the morning.
We see it as rain falling to Earth, too.

Solid ice is another state of water. When it gets cold, water freezes into a solid. We can pack snow to make a snowball. We can catch a snowflake.

We can skate on ice. We can float
ice cubes in lemonade.

Gas is another state of water. We cannot see
water when it is a gas. But it is in the air all
around us. When the gas becomes a liquid,
we see it as a cloud or rain.

When the liquid becomes a solid, we see water as snow or hail.

Water is found in all three states on Earth.
Water can be a solid, a liquid, and a gas.

Can you see all three states of water here?

Review Questions

1. What forms does water take?

2. Where could we find water as a liquid?

3. Where could we find water as a solid (ice)?

4. Where could we find water as a gas?

What Is All around Us?

We can't see it, but it's all around. It's
in the sky. It's in the treetops. It's on the
ground. It's near and far, high and low.
What is it?

Air! We cannot see air, but we know it is there. What happens when you blow up a balloon? You fill it with air. You can see that air takes up space.

You also can feel air on your skin when the **wind** blows. Wind is moving air.

We can tell that air is there when we fly a kite. The wind pushes against the kite and keeps it in the sky.

We can tell that air is there when a parachute floats to the ground. Air pushes up against the parachute so that it comes down slowly.

Even this boat shows us that air is all around. A propeller on the back of the boat pushes on the air. The boat moves forward.

So, what is all around us,
everywhere we go? You know!

Review Questions

1. What does the reading tell us about where air is?

2. How do you know air is there?

3. What other evidence do we have that air is all around us?

4. What is wind?

Weather

Weather is in the air. Sometimes the weather is hot. Sometimes the weather is cold.

Who is dressed for hot weather?
Who is dressed for cold weather?

Sometimes the weather is wet. It can be rainy.
It can be icy. Sometimes the weather is dry.

Who is ready for wet weather?
Who is ready for dry weather?

Sometimes the weather is cloudy.
Sometimes the weather is clear.

Which picture shows a cloudy day?
Which picture shows a clear day?

Sometimes the weather is windy.
Sometimes the weather is calm.

Factories make steam. Which factory shows a
windy day? Which factory shows a calm day?

We can **observe** weather.

We can measure weather.

People use tools to measure weather. Hot and cold weather can be measured with a **thermometer**.

Wet weather can be measured with a **rain gauge**.

Wind direction can be measured
with a **wind sock**.

Trees are in the weather all the time. Trees live
in hot and cold weather. Trees stay calm, or
they move in the wind.

What kind of weather is happening here?

We can **record** weather.

April

Sunday	Monday	Tuesday	Wednesday	Thursday	Friday	Saturday
			1	2	3	4
5	6	7	8	9	10	11
12	13	14	15	16	17	18
19	20	21	22	23	24	25
26	27	28	29	30		

November

Sunday	Monday	Tuesday	Wednesday	Thursday	Friday	Saturday
	1	2	3	4	5	6
7	8	9	10	11	12	13
14	15	16	17	18	19	20
21	22	23	24	25	26	27
28	29	30				

Weather is in the air. You feel and see the weather every day. So go outside. Enjoy the weather.

It might change tomorrow.

Review Questions

1. What do we see when the weather changes?

2. What do we feel when the weather changes?

3. What tools do we use to measure weather?

4. How can we record the weather?

Changes We Observe in the Sky

When you look up at the sky, what do you see? It depends on the time of day. It depends on the time of year, too.

Sometimes you see the Sun. The Sun is a **star** close to Earth. You can feel the Sun's warmth and see it shine. When you can see the Sun's light, it is daytime.

Where do you see the Sun in the morning?
It is low in the sky in the east.

Where do you see the Sun just before it gets dark?
It is low in the sky in the west.

Where do you think
the Sun is at noon?

Where do you see the Sun at night? You can't
see the Sun because it isn't in the night sky. The
sky is dark without the Sun in the sky. The Sun
makes day and night.

When do you see other stars in the sky? You see other stars only at night. It has to be dark to see them.

Here are stars we see in the summer sky and the winter sky. Do they look like the same pattern of stars?

summer

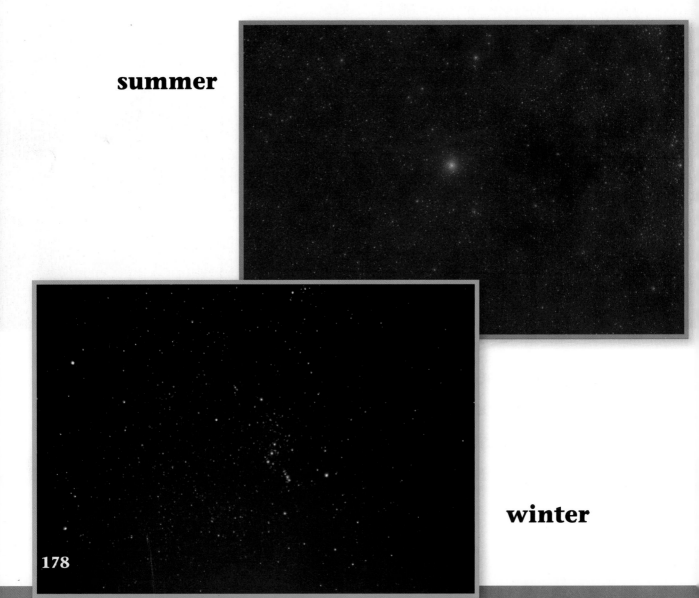

winter

Sometimes you see clouds in the sky.
It is easier to see clouds in the day sky.
But clouds can be in the night sky, too.

Clouds move with the wind. They change
all the time. Sometimes clouds block the Sun.
They make **shadows** on the ground.

Sometimes you see the **Moon** in the sky. You can see the Moon in the day sky and the night sky. But it looks different at different times.

This is a full Moon. You can see a full Moon only at night.

Sometimes the Moon looks like a smile.
This shape is called a crescent Moon. You
can see a crescent Moon in the day sky
and the night sky.

Sometimes the Moon looks like a half circle. This shape is called a quarter Moon. You can see a quarter Moon in the day sky and the night sky.

Sometimes the Moon looks like an egg. This shape is called a gibbous Moon. You can see a gibbous Moon in the day sky and the night sky.

Observe the Moon every day or night for a month. Record what you see and when you see it. Is there a pattern to the Moon shapes you see?

Month _____

Sunday	Monday	Tuesday	Wednesday	Thursday	Friday	Saturday
1	2	3	4	5	6	7
8	9	10	11	12	13	14
15	16	17	18	19	20	21
22	23	24	25	26	27	28

Review Questions

1. When do we see the Sun?

2. What is night?

3. What can we see in the night sky?

4. Think about the Sun, Moon, and stars.
Do they always stay in one place in the sky?
Do they always look the same?

Seasons

In many areas, the **seasons**
bring different kinds of weather.

Fall

Leaves change color and drop from the trees. Squirrels find seeds to eat. A cool wind blows. We put on our sweatshirts to play in the leaves of fall.

Winter

Trees stand bare. Few animals stir. Snow falls to the ground. We bundle up to keep ourselves warm before we go sledding outdoors.

Spring

Leaves grow on trees. Flowers bloom. Birds are building their nests. The air warms up, and we go out to play in the warm, soft breezes of spring.

Summer

The Sun shines brightly on a hot summer day.
There isn't a cloud in the sky. The trees give us
shade. We can make lemonade. Then, we're
off to the beach nearby.

The seasons can make everything look different. Which season do you see in each picture? How can you tell?

Knowing the weather in each season helps us make choices. We can choose what to wear. We can choose to go swimming or skiing. We can decide to walk or drive to the store.

Review Questions

1. What are seasons?

2. What changes the most from season to season?

3. What do we do in different seasons?

Life Science

Plants and Animals

Table of Contents

What Do Plants Need?

Many people grow **plants**. They grow plants in pots and window boxes. They grow plants in gardens and on farms. Farmers grow plants to sell. They know the **basic needs** of plants.

Plants need water. Their **roots** take up
water. Water travels from the roots to the
stems, **leaves**, and flowers.

Plants need **nutrients**. Nutrients come from the soil. Water carries the nutrients through the plants.

Plants need light and **air**. Their
leaves capture light. Green leaves
use **sunlight** and air to make
food. Plants need food to grow.

Plants need space. Roots need space to grow. Crowded roots can't get enough water and nutrients. Crowded leaves can't get enough light.

Does this plant have what it needs to grow?

Review Questions

1. What are the basic needs of plants?

2. What part of a plant takes up water?

3. Where do nutrients come from?

4. What part of a plant captures light?

5. Compare a plant's leaves and flowers. How are they the same? How are they different?

The Story of Wheat

People use plants in many ways. They make clothing and houses from plants. They also use plants for food.

Wheat is an important food plant.
People use wheat to make **flour**.
Flour is used in cooking and baking.

How does wheat grow? First, farmers
sow wheat seeds in big fields.

Soon, the seeds sprout. The wheat looks
like grass. The plants grow bigger and
bigger. Each wheat plant grows new
seeds. The seeds are called **grain**.

The wheat plants dry and turn golden. It's time to **harvest** the wheat grain. The farmer drives a machine called a **combine** over the field. The combine cuts the wheat plant. The combine collects only the grain.

Farmers store the grain in large silos.
Later, it will go to a mill.

But farmers keep some of the grain.
Why do you think they keep some of it?

The mill grinds the grain into flour.
The flour flows into sacks. Bakeries
and grocery stores buy the flour.

Cooks and bakers use flour. They mix it with
water and other things. The mixture might
be baked in an oven. It might be cooked
on a stove. When it's done, there is always
something good to eat!

Bread, pasta, and tortillas are made from flour.
Can you think of other things made from flour?

Review Questions

1. What part of the wheat plant is grain?

2. How does grain become flour?

3. Why do farmers save some of the grain?

4. What foods are made from flour?

How Seeds Travel

How can we make sure plants have
the space they need? Get rid of weeds!
Weeds are unwanted plants.

How do weeds get into gardens?

Most weeds start as seeds. Seeds come
from flowers. First, the seeds get ripe.
Then, they are ready to travel!

Some seeds glide or spin in air. They might land far away. If they land on moist soil, they can grow.

Some seeds are carried by **animals**.
These seeds have little hooks. The
hooks can hold onto an animal's fur.
The seeds go where the animal goes.

Some seeds can even be carried by you!
They can stick to your sweater or shoes.
Some seeds will fall off. When they land
on moist soil, they can sprout and grow.

Birds and squirrels can move seeds, too.
Birds eat berries and fly away. There are
seeds inside the berries. The seeds pass
through the birds. Now the seeds are in
new places!

Squirrels eat seeds, too. They hide acorns to eat
during winter. Lost and forgotten acorns can
grow into oak trees. Seeds travel in many ways.
Now can you tell how weeds get into gardens?

Review Questions

1. How do seeds travel in air?

2. How do seeds with hooks travel?

3. How do birds move seeds?

4. How do squirrels move seeds?

5. How do plants depend on animals?

What Do Animals Need?

Animals live in different **habitats**. Some animals live in water. Others live on land. Some animals live on other animals. But all animals have the same basic needs.

Animals need food. They eat plants and animals. They depend on plants and other animals for food. Animals that eat plants are **herbivores**. Animals that eat other animals are **carnivores**.

Animals need water. Most land animals drink
fresh water. Some animals get water only from
their food. Land animals need air. Air contains
oxygen that animals need to live.

Animals need **shelter**. Shelter protects animals from weather and other animals. Some animals use plants for shelter. Burrows and **nests** are safe places for animals.

A **terrarium** is a small habitat. Worms, snails, insects, and plants can live together in a habitat.

Animals are **living** things. Plants are living things, too. All living things have basic needs. What basic needs does a terrarium provide for plants and animals?

Review Questions

1. What are the basic needs of animals?

2. Why do animals need shelter?

3. Look at the terrarium on page 228. How is it like the one that you made in class?

4. In what ways do animals need plants?

Plants and Animals around the World

Plants and animals have **structures** that help them live in many different habitats. The ocean provides many places for plants and animals to live. What do you see in this saltwater habitat? What structures help them survive?

Many plants live in the **rain forest**. Some rain forest plants are very tall. They grow tall to get the light they need. Short rain forest plants have big leaves. Big leaves are needed to collect enough light in a shady forest.

Frogs and sloths live in rain forests.
This green frog is hard to see on the
green leaves. It catches insects with its
long, sticky tongue. Water rolls right
off the frog's smooth skin. Frogs lay
eggs on wet leaves.

Sloths have strong legs and claws. They move slowly in the tops of trees. They eat leaves from the trees. The baby sloth holds onto its mother. The mother sloth and her baby are safe high in the trees.

Plants grow on the cold **tundra**. Summer
days are long. Tundra plants grow flowers
and make seeds in summer. Winter days are
short. Tundra plants stop growing in winter.

Caribou and lemmings live on the tundra. Caribou eat the short tundra plants during summer. They drink from the many rivers. The caribou's thick fur helps it stay warm. Before winter, caribou travel to a warmer place.

Lemmings stay on the tundra all year. In summer, they eat and store seeds. They make nests with dry grass. Their nests and thick fur keep them warm in winter. Fleas on the lemmings stay warm, too.

Plants grow in hot, dry, windy **deserts**.
Desert plants get lots of light. But they
get very little water.

Cactus plants have long roots. The roots
spread in the desert soil. When it rains,
the roots take up water. Cactus plants
store water in their thick stems.

Lizards and elf owls live in the desert. Lizards **thrive** in the hot Sun. They eat insects. Lizards get water from their food. Lizards have big feet with sharp claws. They can run quickly on sand. They climb on rocks to escape from other animals.

Elf owls do not thrive in the hot Sun. This elf owl uses a cactus for shelter. Elf owls hunt insects in the cool nights. Big eyes help owls see in the dark.

Lots of plants grow in **forests**. Summers are
hot. Winters are cold. Many forest trees and
bushes lose their leaves in fall.

It rains a lot in summer. It snows in winter. There is always water for plants and animals in the forest.

Blue jays and chipmunks live in the forest. Blue jays can fly all over the forest. They fly up into trees to find insects. They fly down to streams for water. Trees provide shelter for blue jays.

Chipmunks live in the forest all year. In fall, they gather nuts. They store the nuts in their burrows. Chipmunks stay in their burrows during winter. Their warm fur and stored nuts help them **survive**.

Grasslands have lots of grass. But they often don't have trees. Summers are warm and sunny. Winters are cold. Rain and snow provide water for plants and animals.

In fall, the grass dies and turns golden. Sometimes, wildfires burn the dry grassland. Fire kills young trees and bushes in the grassland. Now there is more space for new plants. Plants like grasses thrive after a fire.

Prairie dogs and hawks live in grasslands.
Prairie dogs live in tunnels under the ground.
They use their strong, sharp claws to dig
tunnels. They come out to eat grass seeds and
stems. They are always watching for danger.

Hawks soar over the grassland on broad wings. They catch small animals with their strong, sharp talons. Hawks thrive when they catch and eat prairie dogs. Hawks are **predators**.

Water lilies live in ponds. Their roots grow in the mud at the bottom of a pond. In spring, water lilies grow big leaves called pads. The pads rest on the surface and collect sunlight. If a pond freezes, the leaves die. Dead leaves feed the animals living under the ice.

Frogs and perch live in ponds. Frogs can live in water. They can also live out of water. Sometimes they sit on lily pads. They are waiting for insects to eat. Frogs use their long, sticky tongue to catch food. If surprised, frogs leap into the water. They can swim quickly with their strong legs.

Perch can find shelter under lily pads. Their colors and patterns make them hard to see. Perch wait in the shadows for insects to eat. If surprised, perch swim to safety. They move quickly using a broad tail and fins.

Review Questions

1. Without human help, how do certain plants get what they need? How does a cactus get enough water? How does a plant in the rain forest get enough sunlight?

2. What structures help plants grow in certain places?

3. What structures help animals survive in certain places?

4. Can animals use plants to help them survive? How?

Animals and Their Young

Animals live and grow in many different habitats. They get food, water, and shelter from their habitats. They might find shelter in a nest or hole. Animals can move around to get food, water, and shelter.

Many young animals need care. Baby monkeys and hummingbirds cannot feed or clean themselves. Parents feed and clean their young.

This mother lion is cleaning her cub.
A young fox is being groomed, too.

Some **offspring** get their first food from their parents. This young penguin is getting some seafood. Can you see the camel getting milk from its mother?

As the young get older, some parents
teach their offspring how to get food.
Mother grizzly bears teach their cubs
to catch fish. The cub might have to
try many times before catching a fish.

Young ospreys need a safe place to grow.
Ospreys build large, strong nests in high
places. The eggs and baby birds are safe
from predators.

Some spiders shelter their eggs in a strong silk case. What other shelters for young do you see?

259

Some animals hide their babies to keep them safe. A hole in a tree is a good hiding place for baby woodpeckers. Some birds hide their nests in dense bushes.

Some parents carry their offspring to keep them safe. What animals do you see carrying their babies? If there is danger, the parent can move quickly to a safer place.

Young animals need to stay warm. Some mothers keep their babies close. Heat from the mother's body keeps the babies warm. How do other animals keep their young warm?

Young animals learn to walk, climb, and swim like their parents. Moving quickly can help young animals survive. Parents help their young stay away from danger.

Parents care for their offspring in many ways. They make a safe shelter. They teach their young to feed, climb, and swim. Some offspring stay close to their parents. How are these parents caring for their young?

Review Questions

1. How do parents care for their offspring?

2. How do parents keep their young warm?

3. Tell how parents provide food for their offspring.

4. What do young animals do if there is danger?

Life Cycles of Animals

Some animals hatch from eggs. Some animals are born alive. They all grow up to be adults. The adults mate and have babies called offspring.

Every animal goes around the life cycle. *Cycle* means to go around. The life cycle of a robin looks like this.

Robin eggs

Baby robins

Young robin

Adult robin

Trout lay eggs in streams. After 6 to 8 weeks, the eggs hatch. Tiny, fat babies swim out. You can see that they are fish. But they don't look like their parents yet.

For the next year, they grow up little by little.
In 2 years, they are adults. They look just
like their parents. They mate and lay eggs in
streams. Can you describe the trout life cycle?

Frogs lay eggs in water, too. When an egg
hatches, a tadpole swims out. It looks more
like a fish with a big head than a frog. It
doesn't look like its parents yet.

The tadpole eats and grows. In a few weeks, the tadpole starts to change. Its long, flat tail gets shorter. Its legs start to grow.

In a few more weeks, the tadpole has grown into a frog. It looks just like its parents. Can you describe the frog life cycle?

Ducks lay eggs in a nest in a **marsh**. The mother duck sits on the eggs to keep them warm. When they hatch, the babies are fluffy and yellow. The babies are called ducklings. You can see that they are ducks. But they don't look like their parents yet.

The ducklings eat and grow. In a few weeks, they get their brown feathers. In a few months, they are adults. They look just like their parents. In the next year, the adult ducks will mate. They will raise new families of ducklings. Can you describe the duck life cycle?

Mice do not lay eggs. Baby mice grow
inside the mother. The babies are born
alive. Newborn mice are pink, hairless,
and blind. You can see that they are mice.
But they don't look like their parents yet.

In a few days, the babies open their eyes. Their fur starts to grow. In a few months, they will be adults. They will be ready to continue the life cycle. They will have babies of their own. Can you describe the life cycle of mice?

Review Questions

1. Tell about the life cycle of a duck.

2. Tell about the life cycle of a fish.

3. Tell about the life cycle of a frog.

4. How are young animals like their parents? How are they different?

References

Table of Contents

Science Safety Rules

1. Listen carefully to your teacher's instructions. Follow all directions. Ask questions if you don't know what to do.

2. Tell your teacher if you have any allergies.

3. Never put any materials in your mouth. Do not taste anything unless your teacher tells you to do so.

4. Never smell any unknown material. If your teacher tells you to smell something, wave your hand over the material to bring the smell toward your nose.

5. Do not touch your face, mouth, ears, eyes, or nose while working with chemicals, plants, or animals.

6. Always protect your eyes. Wear safety goggles when necessary. Tell your teacher if you wear contact lenses.

7. Always wash your hands with soap and warm water after handling chemicals, plants, or animals.

8. Never mix any chemicals unless your teacher tells you to do so.

9. Report all spills, accidents, and injuries to your teacher.

10. Treat animals with respect, caution, and consideration.

11. Clean up your work space after each investigation.

12. Act responsibly during all science activities.

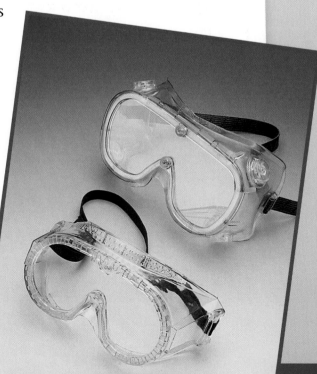

Outdoor Safety Rules

1. Listen carefully to your teacher's instructions. Follow all directions. Ask questions if you don't know what to do.

2. Never put any materials in your mouth.

3. Tell your teacher if you have any allergies. Let your teacher know if you have never been stung by a bee.

4. Dress appropriately for the weather and for the outdoor experience. For long activities in the Sun, wear long sleeves, long pants, and a hat. Use sunscreen.

5. Stay within the designated study area and with your partner or group. When you hear the "freeze" signal, stop and listen to your teacher.

6. Never look directly at the Sun or at the sunlight being reflected off a shiny object.

7. Most plants and animals in the schoolyard are harmless. Know what the skin-irritating plants in your schoolyard look like, and do not touch them. Ask your teacher if you don't know.

8. When looking under a stone or log, lift the side away from you so that any living things can move away from you.

9. If a stinging insect is near you, stay calm and slowly walk away from it. Tell your teacher if you are stung or bitten by any living thing.

10. Take good care of the outdoor environment, and respect all living things. Never release any living things into the environment unless you collected them there.

11. Always wash your hands with soap and warm water after handling plants, animals, and soil.

12. Return to the classroom with all of the materials you brought outside.

Tools for Scientific Investigation

During science class, you use a lot of different tools. These tools help you collect information. They help you record and compare information, too. You use the same tools that scientists do!

Notebooks

This is a notebook. You can use a notebook to record observations, data, and explanations.

Computers

This is a computer. You can use a computer to collect, record, and organize data. A computer can help you compare information, too.

Safety Goggles

This is a pair of safety goggles. You wear safety goggles to protect your eyes while doing science.

Measurement Tools and Rulers

You can use objects as units to compare the length of objects. You can measure the length of a piece of wood by comparing it to the length of a paper clip, a clothespin, or string.

You can use a ruler to measure and compare the length of objects, too.

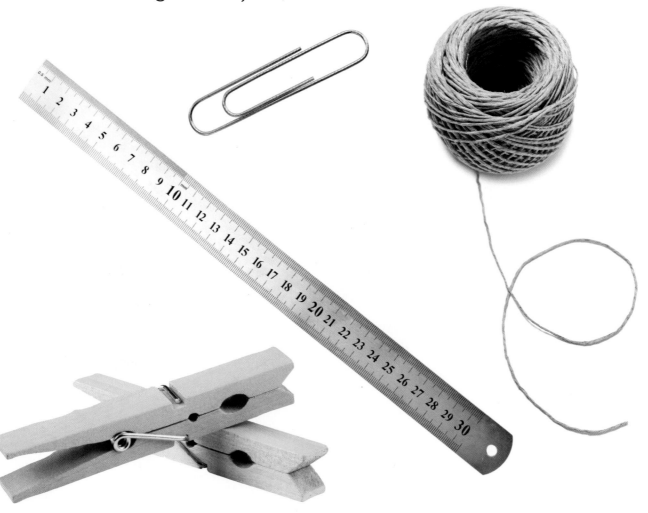

Balances

This is a balance. You can use a balance to compare the weight of two objects. Using standard units, you can measure the mass of a single object.

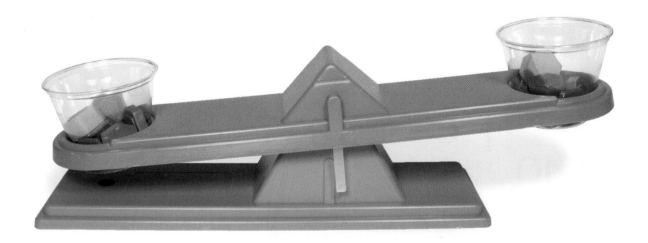

Timing Devices

These are two kinds of devices to keep track of time. You can use a clock or a stopwatch to measure how long it takes for something to happen.

Beakers

This is a beaker. You can use a beaker to measure liquids.

Cups

This is a cup. You can use a cup to collect things, such as rocks and soil samples. You can use a cup to observe things, to mix things, and even to grow plants.

Bowls

This is a container, or bowl. You can use a bowl
to collect things, such as water and pebbles.
You can use a bowl to mix things, too.

Weather Instruments

This is a rain gauge.
A rain gauge measures
rain or snow.

This is a thermometer.
A thermometer measures
temperature.

This is an anemometer. An anemometer
measures wind speed.

Hand Lenses

This is a hand lens. You can use a hand lens to observe living things (plants and animals) and objects up close.

Magnets

These are magnets. You can use a magnet to explore the properties of materials and objects.

Collecting Nets

This is a collecting net. You can use a collecting net to collect small animals from a pond or an aquarium.

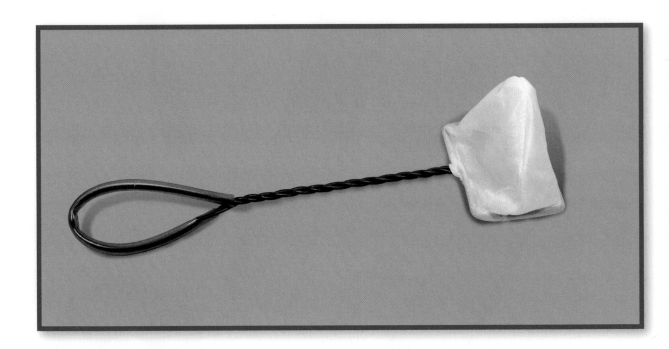

Habitats

This is an aquarium. An aquarium is a small water habitat. You can observe animals and plants in an aquarium.

This is a terrarium. A terrarium is a small land habitat. You can observe plants and animals in a terrarium.

Glossary

air a mixture of gases that we breathe (11, 150, 202)

animal a living thing that is not a plant (218)

asphalt a mixture of pebbles and gravel (107)

axis a straight line around which something turns (70)

basic need something that plants and animals need to survive. Plants need air, water, nutrients, space, and light. Land animals need air, water, food, space, and shelter. (199)

boulder a very large rock that is bigger than a cobble (96)

bubbly describes a liquid that is full of bubbles (46)

carnivore an animal that eats other animals for food (224)

cement a finely ground powder that is like glue when mixed with water (108)

clay rocks that are smaller than sand and silt. It is hard to see just one. (109)

cobble a rock that is smaller than a boulder, but bigger than a pebble (97)

combine a machine that cuts wheat and separates the grain (209)

concrete a mixture of gravel, sand, cement, and water (108)

cool to make something colder (61)

crystal the shape of salt after evaporation (55)

decay when dead plants or animals break down into small pieces (121)

desert a dry place with little rain **(237)**

dissolve when a solid is mixed with a liquid, and the solid breaks apart into pieces so tiny they can't be seen in the liquid **(54)**

evaporate when a liquid dries up, goes into the air as a gas, and can't be seen **(55)**

fabric a flexible material used to make clothing. Fabric and cloth are the same. **(18)**

flour a fine powder made from grinding wheat seeds **(207)**

foamy describes a liquid that has a layer of bubbles on top **(46)**

food what plants and animals need to survive **(202)**

forest a place with many trees and other plants. Many plants in a forest lose their leaves in fall. **(136, 241)**

freeze to change a liquid to a solid by cooling it **(61)**

fresh water water without salt. Fresh water is found in streams, lakes, and rivers. **(131)**

gas matter that can't be seen but is all around. Air is an example of a gas. **(10, 145)**

grain a hard seed that grows on a wheat plant **(208)**

granite the name of a kind of rock. Pink granite is made of four minerals. Those minerals are hornblende (black), mica (black), feldspar (pink), and quartz (gray). **(94)**

grassland a place with a lot of grass and often no trees **(245)**

gravel a rock that is smaller than a pebble, but bigger than sand **(98)**

gravity a force that pulls things toward Earth **(72)**

habitat the place or natural area where plants and animals live **(223)**

harvest to gather a crop, such as wheat **(209)**

heat to make something warmer **(60)**

herbivore an animal that eats plants for food **(224)**

humus bits of dead plant and animal parts in the soil **(121)**

leaf a structure on a plant that is usually green and makes food from sunlight **(200)**

liquid matter that flows freely and takes the shape of its container **(10, 141)**

living alive. All living things have basic needs and produce offspring. **(228)**

magnet an object that sticks to iron and steel. Magnets can push or pull other magnets or objects made of iron or steel. **(65)**

magnetism a force that can work on another object without touching it **(65)**

marsh soft, wet land that is sometimes covered with water **(135, 272)**

material what something is made of **(17)**

matter anything that takes up space **(9)**

melt to change a solid to a liquid by heating it **(59)**

mineral the colorful ingredient that makes up rocks **(92)**

mixture two or more materials put together **(51)**

Moon the object we see in the night sky and sometimes during the day. Some of the Moon shapes we observe and describe are the full Moon, crescent Moon, quarter Moon, and gibbous Moon. **(181)**

mortar a mixture of cement and sand **(111)**

natural resource something from Earth. Rocks, soil, air, and water are natural resources. **(114)**

nest a safe place where animals live and raise their young. Some animals use plants or other animals for nests. **(226)**

nutrient something that living things need to grow and stay healthy **(121, 201)**

object a solid thing **(16)**

observe to use the senses to learn about something **(165)**

offspring a new plant or animal produced by a parent **(256)**

oxygen a gas in air that plants and animals need to live **(225)**

particle a tiny piece of a material **(37)**

pebble a rock that is smaller than a cobble, but bigger than gravel **(97)**

plant a living thing that has roots, stems, and leaves. Plants make their own food. **(199)**

predator an animal that hunts and catches other animals for food **(248)**

predict to make a guess based on previous patterns and information **(59)**

property something that you can observe about an object or a material. Size, color, shape, texture, and smell are properties. **(18, 83)**

rain forest a warm, wet place with many trees and other plants **(231)**

rain gauge a weather tool used to measure rain **(167)**

record to write down information or date **(170)**

retain to hold **(121)**

rock a solid earth material. Rocks are made of minerals. **(83)**

roll to move from one place to another by turning over and over **(69)**

root a part of a plant that grows in soil **(200)**

salt water water with salt. Salt water is found in seas and the ocean. **(134)**

sand rocks that are smaller than gravel, but bigger than silt **(86)**

season one of four times of year that has different weather. Winter, spring, summer, and fall are seasons. **(187)**

shadow a dark area made by blocking the light from the Sun **(180)**

shelter a safe place where animals live. A shelter protects an animal from weather or other animals. **(226)**

silt rocks that are smaller than sand, but bigger than clay **(120)**

sink to fall or drop to the bottom **(38)**

soil a mix of sand, silt, clay, gravel, pebbles, and humus **(120)**

solid matter that holds its own shape and always takes up the same amount of space **(10, 143)**

sow to plant a seed **(207)**

spin to move by turning around an axis **(70)**

star an object in the sky that makes light and heat **(174)**

state one of the three groups of matter: solid, liquid, or gas **(10)**

structure any part of a plant or animal that can be named **(230)**

sunlight something plants need to make food **(202)**

surface the top layer of something **(38)**

survive to stay alive **(244)**

terrarium a small container with soil where plants and animals can live **(227)**

texture the way something feels **(90)**

thermometer a weather tool used to measure temperature **(166)**

thrive to grow fast and stay healthy **(239)**

tower a tall structure **(25)**

translucent describes a liquid or solid that is clear enough to let light through but is not clear enough to see something on the other side **(46)**

transparent describes a liquid or solid that you can see through easily **(46)**

tundra a place in the arctic or high on mountains **(234)**

viscous describes a liquid that is thick and slow moving **(46)**

weather the condition of the air outdoors **(157)**

weathering when rocks break apart over time to become smaller and smaller **(99)**

wheat a type of grass that makes seeds that can be ground into flour **(207)**

wind moving air **(151)**

wind sock a weather tool used to measure wind direction **(168)**

304